MW01147546

BY THOMAS K. ADAMSON

THE TENNESSEE
TITANS
STORY

BELLWETHER MEDIA · MINNEAPOLIS, MN

TM

Are you ready to take it to the extreme? Torque books thrust you into the action-packed world of sports, vehicles, mystery, and adventure. These books may include dirt, smoke, fire, and chilling tales. **WARNING**: read at your own risk.

This edition first published in 2017 by Bellwether Media, Inc.

No part of this publication may be reproduced in whole or in part without written permission of the publisher. For information regarding permission, write to Bellwether Media, Inc., Attention: Permissions Department, 5357 Penn Avenue South, Minneapolis, MN 55419.

Library of Congress Cataloging-in-Publication Data

Names: Adamson, Thomas K., 1970- author.
Title: The Tennessee Titans Story / by Thomas K. Adamson.
Description: Minneapolis, MN : Bellwether Media, Inc., 2017. | Series:
  Torque: NFL teams | Includes bibliographical references and index.
Identifiers: LCCN 2016010452 | ISBN 9781626173859 (hardcover : alk. paper)
Subjects: LCSH: Tennessee Titans (Football team)–History–Juvenile literature.
Classification: LCC GV956.T45 A34 2017 | DDC 796.332/640976855–dc23
LC record available at https://lccn.loc.gov/2016010452

Text copyright © 2017 by Bellwether Media, Inc. TORQUE and associated logos are trademarks and/or registered trademarks of Bellwether Media, Inc.

SCHOLASTIC, CHILDREN'S PRESS, and associated logos are trademarks and/or registered trademarks of Scholastic Inc.

Printed in the United States of America, North Mankato, MN.

TABLE OF CONTENTS

The Tennessee Titans face the Pittsburgh Steelers on December 21, 2008. In the third quarter, the Steelers lead 14 to 10.

Kerry Collins

Jeff Fisher

The Titans have a chance to kick a field goal to score three more points. But instead of trying for a field goal, head coach Jeff Fisher makes a bold decision. He says to go for a touchdown!

Chris Johnson

The Titans' **quarterback** flips the ball to **running back** Chris Johnson. The daring play surprises Pittsburgh's **defense**. Johnson runs the ball 21 yards for a touchdown!

Then, the Titans add two more touchdowns. They win home-field advantage for the **playoffs**.

SCORING TERMS

END ZONE

the area at each end of a football field; a team scores by entering the opponent's end zone with the football.

EXTRA POINT

a score that occurs when a kicker kicks the ball between the opponent's goal posts after a touchdown is scored; 1 point.

FIELD GOAL

a score that occurs when a kicker kicks the ball between the opponent's goal posts; 3 points.

SAFETY

a score that occurs when a player on offense is tackled behind his own goal line; 2 points for defense.

TOUCHDOWN

a score that occurs when a team crosses into its opponent's end zone with the football; 6 points.

TWO-POINT CONVERSION

a score that occurs when a team crosses into its opponent's end zone with the football after scoring a touchdown; 2 points.

7

The Titans are Tennessee's first and only National Football League (NFL) team. One of their most memorable moments was the "Music City Miracle" play in 2000.

Kevin Dyson

The Titans were behind in a playoff game. In the last three seconds, a Titans player made an unusual **lateral** pass. **Wide receiver** Kevin Dyson ran 75 yards for a touchdown!

The Titans play home games at Nissan Stadium in Nashville, Tennessee. The Titans began playing there in 1999. In this open, outdoor stadium, every fan has a good view of the game.

STADIUM MAKEOVER

In 2012, huge video boards were added above each end zone of Nissan Stadium. Later, all of the seats were replaced with new ones.

NASHVILLE, TENNESSEE

The NFL has 32 football teams. Each plays in a **conference** and **division**. The Titans play in the South Division of the American Football Conference (AFC).

The other three AFC South teams are their **rivals**. Games against the Indianapolis Colts are especially wild.

NFL DIVISIONS

 **AFC**

AFC NORTH

BALTIMORE **RAVENS**	CINCINNATI **BENGALS**
CLEVELAND **BROWNS**	PITTSBURGH **STEELERS**

AFC EAST

BUFFALO **BILLS**	MIAMI **DOLPHINS**
PATRIOTS	NEW YORK **JETS**

AFC SOUTH

HOUSTON **TEXANS**	INDIANAPOLIS **COLTS**
JACKSONVILLE **JAGUARS**	TENNESSEE **TITANS**

AFC WEST

DENVER **BRONCOS**	KANSAS CITY **CHIEFS**
RAIDERS OAKLAND	SAN DIEGO **CHARGERS**

RIVAL MVPs

In 2003, the Titans' Steve McNair and the Colts' Peyton Manning tied for the NFL's Most Valuable Player (MVP).

NFC

NFC NORTH

CHICAGO
BEARS

DETROIT
LIONS

GREEN BAY
PACKERS

MINNESOTA
VIKINGS

NFC EAST

DALLAS
COWBOYS

GIANTS

PHILADELPHIA
EAGLES

WASHINGTON
REDSKINS

NFC SOUTH

FALCONS

CAROLINA
PANTHERS

NEW ORLEANS
SAINTS

BUCCANEERS

NFC WEST

CARDINALS

LOS ANGELES
RAMS

SAN FRANCISCO
49ERS

SEATTLE
SEAHAWKS

Tennessee has not always been the Titans' home. In 1960, the team started in Texas as the Houston Oilers. They won the first two American Football League (AFL) Championships for the 1960 and 1961 seasons.

The Oilers joined the NFL in 1970 when the leagues **merged**. They were a strong team in the late 1970s.

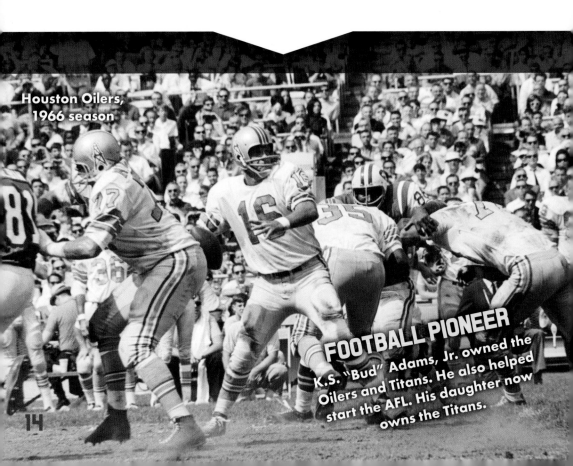

Houston Oilers, 1966 season

FOOTBALL PIONEER
K.S. "Bud" Adams, Jr. owned the Oilers and Titans. He also helped start the AFL. His daughter now owns the Titans.

Houston Oilers, 1980s

Earl Campbell

By the 1990s, team owner Bud Adams wanted a new stadium. Leaders in Nashville agreed to build one for the Oilers. The team moved to Tennessee in 1997. There, they won people's hearts.

Bud Adams

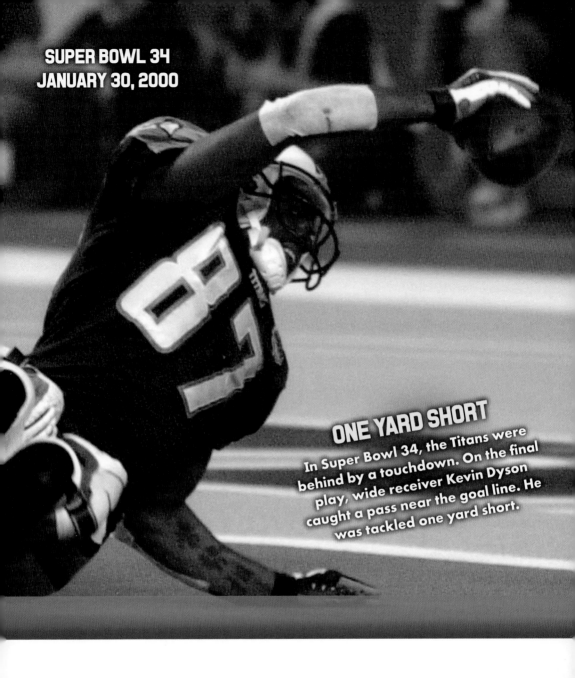

ONE YARD SHORT

In Super Bowl 34, the Titans were behind by a touchdown. On the final play, wide receiver Kevin Dyson caught a pass near the goal line. He was tackled one yard short.

Two years later, their new stadium opened, and they were renamed the Titans. They went all the way to **Super Bowl** 34 that season.

TIMELINE

1960

First played as the Houston Oilers in the AFL

1961

Won first-ever AFL Championship for the 1960 season

1997

Moved to Tennessee

1970

Joined the NFL as an AFC Central team

1999

First played as the Tennessee Titans at Nissan Stadium in Nashville

1961

Won AFL Championship for the 1961 season, beating the San Diego Chargers (10-3)

2000

Won the "Music City Miracle" playoff game, beating the Buffalo Bills (22-16)

2004

Celebrated Steve McNair being named the NFL's co-MVP for the 2003 season

2000

Won the AFC Championship for the 1999 season, beating the Jacksonville Jaguars (33-14)

2002

Moved to the AFC South

2010

Celebrated running back Chris Johnson setting a new single-season rushing record with 2,509 yards from scrimmage

George Blanda was the team's first quarterback. He was also the **kicker**. He led the team to two AFL Championships.

George Blanda

AGELESS PLAYER

George Blanda played an amazing 26 seasons of professional football! He has the longest career of any football player.

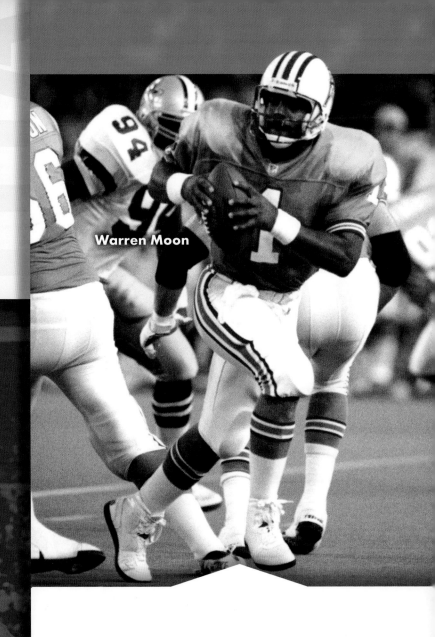

Warren Moon

Warren Moon was also
a talented quarterback.
He set a team record for
passing. Moon threw for
more than 33,000 yards!

Running back Earl
Campbell was the NFL's MVP
for 1979. He led the NFL
in **rushing yards** during
his first three seasons. Bruce
Matthews was one of the
best **offensive linemen**
in the game. He made 14
Pro Bowl appearances.

On defense, Elvin Bethea
was one of the great pass
rushers of the 1970s.
He is the team's all-time
sack leader.

TEAM GREATS

GEORGE BLANDA
QUARTERBACK, KICKER
1960-1966

ELVIN BETHEA
DEFENSIVE END
1968-1983

EARL CAMPBELL
RUNNING BACK
1978-1984

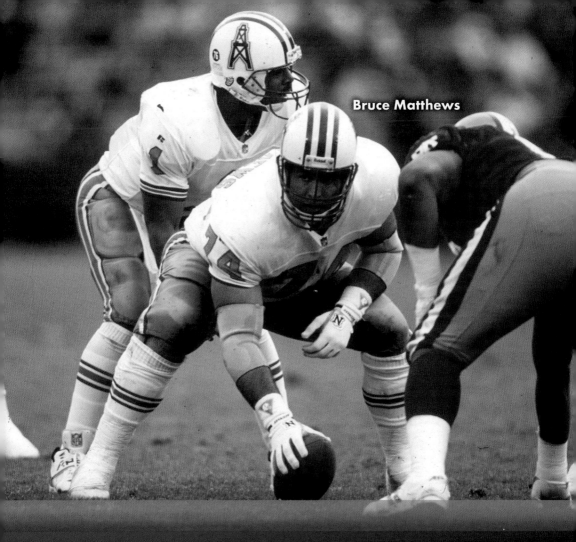

Bruce Matthews

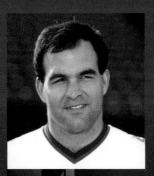

BRUCE MATTHEWS
OFFENSIVE LINEMAN
1983-2001

WARREN MOON
QUARTERBACK
1984-1993

STEVE McNAIR
QUARTERBACK
1995-2005

When the Titans changed their name,
they updated their team logo, colors, and
uniforms. But they did not entirely forget
their roots.

The Titans still have a light blue color. It is similar to the shade of blue that was used by the Houston Oilers.

HUGE AND POWERFUL
The word *titan* comes from Greek stories and myths. Titans were powerful giants.

The changes brought on a new age for the Titans. It was a fresh start for players and fans alike.

T-Rac

Whether making huge single plays, or beating rivals on the field, Titans football remains exciting. Fans await a return to a championship game!

MORE ABOUT THE

TITANS

Team name:
Tennessee Titans

Team name explained:
Named to reflect strong, heroic qualities

Conference: **AFC**

Division: **South**

Main rivals: **Indianapolis Colts, Jacksonville Jaguars**

Joined NFL: **1970**
(AFL from 1960-1969)

Hometown:
Nashville, Tennessee

Training camp location:
Saint Thomas Sports Park, Nashville, Tennessee

N
W — E
S

NASHVILLE

TENNESSEE

Home stadium name: Nissan Stadium

Stadium opened: 1999

Seats in stadium: 69,143

Logo: A silver capital T surrounded by a navy circle and three red stars; red and blue flames trail off the circle to the upper left.

Colors: Light blue, navy, red, silver

Mascot: T-Rac

29

GLOSSARY

conference—a large grouping of sports teams that often play one another

defense—the group of players who try to stop the opposing team from scoring

division—a small grouping of sports teams that often play one another; usually there are several divisions of teams in a conference.

kicker—a player whose main job is to kick extra points, field goals, and kickoffs

lateral—sideways; a lateral pass is thrown sideways or backward instead of forward.

merged—combined two things into one

offensive linemen—players on offense whose main jobs are to protect the quarterback and to block for running backs

playoffs—the games played after the regular NFL season is over; playoff games determine which teams play in the Super Bowl.

Pro Bowl—an all-star game played after the regular season in which the best players in the NFL face one another

quarterback—a player on offense whose main job is to throw and hand off the ball

rivals—teams that are long-standing opponents

running back—a player on offense whose main job is to run with the ball

rushing yards—yards gained by running with the ball

sack—to tackle the opposing quarterback for a loss of yards

Super Bowl—the championship game for the NFL

wide receiver—a player on offense whose main job is to catch passes from the quarterback

TO LEARN MORE

AT THE LIBRARY

Gilbert, Sara. *The Story of the Tennessee Titans.* Mankato, Minn.: Creative Education, 2014.

Stewart, Mark. *The Tennessee Titans.* Chicago, Ill.: Norwood House Press, 2013.

Wyner, Zach. *Tennessee Titans.* New York, N.Y.: AV2 by Weigl, 2015.

ON THE WEB

Learning more about the Tennessee Titans is as easy as 1, 2, 3.

1. Go to www.factsurfer.com.

2. Enter "Tennessee Titans" into the search box.

3. Click the "Surf" button and you will see a list of related web sites.

With factsurfer.com, finding more information is just a click away.

INDEX

The images in this book are reproduced through the courtesy of: Corbis, front cover (large, small), pp. 4-5, 14, 19 (top right), 22 (right), 28; M. J. Masotti Jr./ Reuters/ Newscom, p. 5; Rex Brown/ Getty Images, pp. 6-7; John Russell/ AP Images, p. 7; Allen Kee/ Getty Images, pp. 8-9; Weston Kenney/ AP Images, pp. 10-11; Mark Zaleski/ AP Images, p. 11; Michael Zito/ SportsChrome/ Newscom, pp. 12-13; Deposit Photos/ Glow Images, pp. 12-13 (logos), 18-19 (logos), 28-29 (logos); NFL Photos/ AP Images, pp. 15, 18 (top), 22 (middle), 23 (middle); Wade Payne/ AP Images, p. 16; Mark Humphrey/ AP Images, pp. 16-17; Pro Football Hall of Fame/ AP Images, p. 18 (bottom); Al Messerschmidt/ AP Images, p. 19 (top left); Larry W. Smith/ EPA/ Newscom, p. 19 (bottom); AP Images, pp. 20-21, 22 (left); Atsushi Tsukada/ AP Images, p. 21; Joseph Patronite/ Getty Images, pp. 22-23; Paul Spinelli/ AP Images, pp. 23 (left), 29 (mascot); Scott Boehm/ AP Images, p. 23 (right); James Kenney/ AP Images, p. 24; Frederick Breedon/ AP Images, p. 25; Greg McWilliams/ Icon SMI/ Newscom, p. 26; ZUMA Press/ Alamy, pp. 26-27; Chris Upchurch/ Dreamstime, p. 29 (stadium).